RAND NATIONAL DEFENSE RESEARCH INSTITUTE

# The Millennial Generation

## Implications for the Intelligence and Policy Communities

Cortney Weinbaum, Richard Girven, Jenny Oberholtzer

Prepared for the Office of the Secretary of Defense

For more information on this publication, visit www.rand.org/t/RR1306

Library of Congress Cataloging-in-Publication Data
ISBN: 978-0-8330-9421-6

Published by the RAND Corporation, Santa Monica, Calif.

© Copyright 2016 RAND Corporation

RAND® is a registered trademark.

Cover: FotolEdhar/Fotolia

### Support RAND

Make a tax-deductible charitable contribution at
www.rand.org/giving/contribute

www.rand.org

# Preface

Millennials are challenging the status quo and changing the shape of U.S. government workplaces. This generational shift is disrupting long-standing recruiting, hiring, education, and sustainment practices for companies and forcing reevaluations of enterprise information technology investments and known career paths.

This report fills a gap that previous surveys, studies, reports, and discussions on millennials had left by describing how the intelligence community (IC) must engage millennials across multiple segments to succeed in the future. Here, we examine four segments of millennials with which the IC will need to engage in the future: intelligence clients, employees, and partners and members of the public. We explore how the perspectives and experiences of millennials falling into each segment are relevant to IC functions and missions. Millennials in each segment may perceive intelligence differently than previous generations, which may influence whether and how they partner and engage with the IC; such decisions will affect future intelligence missions. This report provides an understanding of areas in which intelligence agencies may benefit from further study.

This research was conducted within the Intelligence Policy Center of the RAND National Defense Research Institute, a federally funded research and development center sponsored by the Office of the Secretary of Defense, the Joint Staff, the Unified Combatant Commands, the Navy, the Marine Corps, the defense agencies, and the defense Intelligence Community.

For more information on the Intelligence Policy Center, see http://www.rand.org/nsrd/ndri/centers/intel.html or contact the director (contact information is provided on the web page).

# Contents

# Figures and Boxes

## Figures

## Boxes

# Summary

In 2015, for the first time, millennials outnumbered baby boomers as the largest generational segment of the U.S. population. As baby boomers exit the workforce, new millennials will also continue to immigrate to the United States, continuing to grow the divide between these two populations' workforce sizes. The U.S. intelligence community's (IC's) mission demands that its agencies attract premier employees, capable of tackling complex problems with creativity, analytical thinking, and insight across diverse disciplines. The success of such a workforce requires information-sharing partnerships with foreign governments, foreign nationals, and U.S. industry partners. In all these groups, millennials will be found in increasingly senior leadership positions. Tomorrow's intelligence consumers, the policymakers and decisionmakers who will rely on timely and accurate intelligence to do their jobs, will also be millennials. The IC must engage this generation for intelligence to remain relevant to U.S. policy decisions in the future.

Many surveys and studies exist on millennials in the U.S. workforce at large, the perceptions millennials have about government and other industries, and how millennials' attitudes and outlooks vary by country. These studies often contrast millennials' viewpoints with those of other generations. Yet never before has this information been applied to the unique missions and functions of intelligence agencies, and the roles millennials must play—inside and outside these agencies—for the agencies to succeed at their missions. In addition to a lack of analysis applying existing research to this topic, research specific to millennials and intelligence is lacking. Research suggests that generational differences detected in other sectors will be relevant in the IC. While this report explores such relevant topics, no known research has explored why some U.S. millennials choose not to apply for intelligence jobs and which competencies the IC workforce lacks as a result.

Meanwhile, millennials outside the IC are rising in military ranks and policy roles, taking on greater policy and decisionmaking responsibilities and thereby becoming intelligence consumers. These consumers access and interact with information differently from their predecessors, expecting around the clock, real-time, access to information anywhere they are. Millennials are being elected to legislative positions; as committee members in Congress, millennials will decide on budget authorizations and other laws that directly affect the ability of intelligence agencies to conduct their missions. Millennial lawmakers do not assume that government "business as usual" is necessarily the best approach for their constituents and may be reluctant to approve bills without asking why specific programs are needed at the requested funding levels.

This environment may feel complicated for IC agencies to navigate, but unfortunately the complexities of government are straightforward compared to the demands the public can make. For the first time in decades, the IC finds itself in a position in which public perception in both the United States and abroad has immediate and severe effects on agencies' abilities to conduct their missions. Concerns about how data are collected, stored, used, and shared have led many millennials—in the United States and in foreign countries—to question the role of intelligence and to be vocal about their concerns when interacting with the political leaders who have the authority to affect programs and partnership agreements.

The concerns foreign millennials have about U.S. intelligence have become urgent because the IC *needs* these millennials. Foreign millennials are rising into decision-making, military leadership, and government and nongovernmental positions in which they will decide on liaison sharing agreements and become desired sources for intelligence. If these millennials do not believe that partnering with the U.S. government is in their countries' best interests, the IC may encounter critical intelligence gaps in the future.

We reviewed available research on millennials in the United States and abroad and surveys of the IC workforce to assess how the millennial generation may affect intelligence and how the IC can improve its engagement of this generation. We divided the millennial population into four segments to analyze from the IC perspective: the public, clients, IC employees, and the IC "gene pool." The gene pool consists of contractors, researchers, foreign liaisons, and other millennials who interact with the IC but do not fit into the other three segments. We learned that, across these segments, millennials in each country are motivated by different goals that are shaped by local needs and that the IC should engage millennials differently based on their local goals, expectations, and concerns. Further, the IC needs different things from each segment and should therefore engage each differently. For example, the IC will need to establish a different outreach and intelligence sharing relationship with a millennial in Congress from the one it would establish with a millennial in a foreign government and should therefore tailor communications, outreach, and expectations accordingly.

Until this report, no assessment or analysis of millennials' roles in intelligence existed. We further discovered a lack of research on how millennials' perceptions of the IC differ from those of other generations. The IC will need the contributions of millennials from all four segments—members of the public, clients, IC employees, and IC gene pool members. We have therefore sought to provide an understanding of *why* engaging millennials in these segments will differ from engaging previous generations. At the same time, however, we found insufficient data to examine and comprehensively understand *how* to engage millennials across the four segments in intelligence. We found evidence that millennials in the United States simultaneously lack trust in the federal government yet believe that the government has the responsibility and ability to respond to war, terrorism, social unrest, cyber security, and political instability. This dichotomy provides an opportunity for intelligence agencies to explore in determining how to engage with this demographic in ways that are productive to national security missions.

# CHAPTER ONE

# Introduction

This report presents a preliminary exploration of how the millennial generation will affect the intelligence and policy communities as producers of and advisors on intelligence and as policymakers. We sought to identify themes about millennials that may affect the ability of intelligence agencies to conduct their missions and to determine whether additional research is warranted.

We define millennials as people born from 1980 through 2004, who would have been 12 to 36 years old in 2016 (see Figure 1.1).[1] Millennials are challenging the status quo and changing the shape of U.S. government workplaces. This generational shift is disrupting long-standing recruiting, hiring, education, and sustainment practices for companies and is forcing reevaluations of enterprise information technology (IT) investments and known career paths. In addition to the roles millennials have in the IC workforce, we considered the roles millennials play as intelligence consumers, foreign liaisons, intelligence sources, and partners across the research, academic, and commercial sectors. The IC's ability to engage and partner with millennials outside agency workforces will determine the future success of intelligence.

## Why Millennials Matter to Intelligence

> We are together in a disdain for the status quo. We are together in our lack of appreciation for processes instead of outcomes, and we are together that while we may have strong principled views that vary, that we also believe we grew up in a society where you don't get everything you want.
>
> —*Rep. Aaron Schock (R-Ill.), age 33*[2]

---

[1] We have used the most inclusive definition, although various studies have defined the millennial generation differently. For example, Strauss and Howe uses 1984–2004; Pew Research Trust uses 1981–1998; McCrindle Research Center uses 1980–1994. See William Strauss and Neil Howe, *Millennials Rising: The Next Great Generation*, New York: Vintage Books, 2000; Pew Research Center, *Millennials: A Portrait of Generation Next: Confident. Connected. Open to Change*, Washington, D.C., February 2010; Mark McCrindle, "Superannuation and the Under 40s," summary report, Bella Vista NSW, Australia: McCrindle Research, July 18, 2005.

[2] Representative Schock was also speaking of Rep. Tulsi Gabbard (D-Hawaii), also age 33 (Stephanie Czekalinski and Ronald Brownstein, "What It's Like to Be a Millennial in Congress," *National Journal*, June 5, 2014).

**Figure 1.1**
**Projected Population, by Generation**

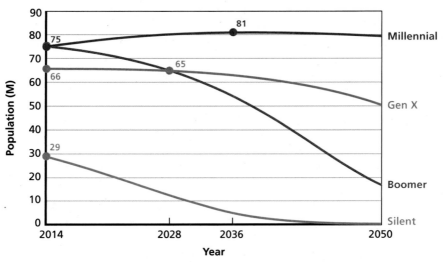

SOURCE: Richard Fry, "Millennials Overtake Baby Boomers as America's Largest
Generation," Pew Research Center website, April 25, 2016. Data from Pew Research
Center tabulations of U.S. Census Bureau population projections dated December
2014. Used with permission.
NOTE: The term millennials encompasses those aged 18–34 in 2015.
**RAND** *RR11306-2.1*

In the intelligence community (IC), millennials constitute much of the non–Senior
Executive Service workforce and the entire entry-level labor market that the IC intends
to recruit for the next 10 years. In the United States, members of this generation are
already rising into policy and decisionmaking roles that place them at the center of
the IC's consumer market. In 2015, two millennials were elected to Congress and
thus now have voting rights on legislation and budget authorizations that affect the
IC.[3] Eventually, this generation will have seats on all the IC's congressional oversight
committees. Millennials already fill essential positions as contractors across all 17 intelligence agencies and are among the scientists and researchers developing future innovations that will change intelligence collection, processing, exploitation and analysis.
In foreign countries, millennials are rising in the ranks of the North Atlantic Treaty
Organization (NATO), other liaison partners, and adversaries.[4]

Globally, millennials constitute the most educated, most informed, and most
interconnected generation in history, making them highly desirable employees and

---

[3]   Czekalinski and Brownstein, 2014.

[4]   Not every country uses the term *millennial*, but we use it here to describe anyone on the planet born between
1980–2004, even though specific countries or cultures may use a different term for people born in this period.

business partners for the IC.[5] One survey of millennials born 1981–1993 found that "61% are worried about the state of the world and feel personally responsible to make a difference. . . . This generation is worried about the world on a broad scale, and expects companies to support major world issues."[6]

In some foreign countries, millennials are rising through the ranks of governments as fast as they are in the United States. In Canada, for example, seven millennials, ages 19 and up, were elected to Parliament in 2011.[7] Millennials are helping to shape their regions and communities wherever they reside. Millennials were participants in the Arab Spring movements that spread across the Middle East in 2010 and were prominent among anti-Japan protesters in multiple Chinese cities in 2012.[8]

The ability of IC agencies to partner with this generation at home and abroad will determine the future of intelligence collection capabilities, information sharing, net technological innovations, and workforce retention and development, among others.

In the United States, 9/11 may have been a call to action that brought some millennials into the IC as civilians, military service members, or contractors. Yet younger millennials have no memories of the United States before 9/11 because they were either small children or had not yet been born in 2001. For these younger millennial Americans, the "War on Terror" has always existed, and the United States has always been at war in the Middle East and South Asia. While many Americans over the age of 35 who grew up in middle- or upper-class neighborhoods remember schools as being sanctuaries for learning, millennials have always lived with the threat of school shootings and massacres, including the events at Columbine High School in 1999, Virginia Tech in 2007, and Sandy Hook Elementary School in 2012. This generation has few illusions about government or big business; it has witnessed the worst of corporate greed through Enron, Arthur Andersen, and the subprime mortgage crisis. And millennials have watched their fellow citizens lose faith and trust in government following the Snowden leaks in 2013 and congressional investigations into the events in Benghazi in 2012 and the Central Intelligence Agency's (CIA's) detention and interrogation program.

While members of this generation may feel that their government and corporations are unable to protect them—from school violence, transnational terrorism, or

---

[5]  Victoria Stilwell, "Millennials Most-Educated U.S. Age Group After Downturn: Economy," Bloomberg Markets website October 8, 2014.

[6]  Cone Inc., "The Millennial Generation: Pro-Social and Empowered to Change the World," 2006.

[7]  Diane Brady, "Millennials Descend on Canada's Parliament," *Bloomberg Businessweek*, May 19, 2011.

[8]  Juan Cole, *The New Arabs: How the Millennial Generation Is Changing the Middle East*, New York: Simon & Schuster, 2014; Eric Fish, *China's Millennials: The Want Generation,* Lanham, Md.: Rowman & Littlefield, June 4, 2015, pp. 56–59.

financial greed—they also feel a responsibility to improve both the public and private sectors and believe the sectors should work together to solve hard problems.[9]

Millennials are the first generation to have been born into households with personal computers and to have been raised in an environment of continuous exposure to digital media.[10] Millennials are technologically savvy and are connected to online news, entertainment, and social information networks. As they did throughout high school and college, millennials will continue to rely on having access 24 hours a day, seven days a week through smart phones, personal electronic devices, and computers.[11] Increasingly, millennials are preferring new media (via the Internet, including social media) over conventional media (television, newspapers, and magazines) as their best sources of credible news coverage in general or for news on a developing story or crisis. Only 24 percent of millennials say they get most of their news from a newspaper, while 59 percent rely on the Internet for news.[12] Mobile phones, especially smart phones, are increasingly the most important technological device in millennials' lives:

> The internet and mobile phones have been broadly adopted in America in the past 15 years, and Millennials have been leading technology enthusiasts. For them, these innovations provide more than a bottomless source of information and entertainment, and more than a new ecosystem for their social lives. They also are a badge of generational identity. Many Millennials say their use of modern technology is what distinguishes them from other generations.[13]

Millennials, who are continuously connected to news and social media, also prefer open communication and continuous feedback throughout the organizations and teams in which they participate.[14] They prefer quick responses to questions, have an urgent sense of immediacy, and get impatient with the slow pace of organizations that are less than cutting edge in their usage of technology.[15] Once they have information, they want to share and discuss it. Millennials are unlikely to readily accept

---

[9]  Deloitte, "Big Demands and High Expectations: The Deloitte Millennial Survey—Executive Summary," New York, January 2014, p. 3.

[10]  Phil Gorman, Teresa Nelson, and Alan Glassman, "The Millennial Generation: A Strategic Opportunity," *Organizational Analysis*, Vol. 12, No. 3, July 2004, pp. 255–270.

[11]  Telefónica, "Global Millennial Survey: Global Results," website, 2013a.

[12]  Pew Research Center, 2010, p. 35.

[13]  Pew Research Center, 2010.

[14]  Carol A. Martin, "From High Maintenance to High Productivity: What Managers Need to Know About Generation Y," *Industrial and Commercial Training*, Vol. 37, No. 1, 2005.

[15]  Martin, 2005, p. 41.

organizational policies that limit the sharing of information, a tendency that is directly contrary to the IC's "need to know" policy and mindset.[16]

## Intelligence in a Changing World

The United States and its allies continue to face a highly complex and ever-changing global security environment characterized by extremely dangerous, pervasive, and sometimes elusive threats. While the world has always been a dangerous place, and every generation faces difficult new challenges and crises, many intelligence professionals describe contemporary threats as more prevalent and varied than at any time in recorded history. As Director of National Intelligence James Clapper testified in open testimony before the Senate Select Committee on Intelligence in 2014: "Looking back over my more than half a century in intelligence, I've not experienced a time when we've been beset by more crises and threats around the globe."[17]

While core al-Qa'ida declines in strength and global reach, the Islamic State has created human devastation in Iraq and Syria while promoting a violent ideology that has inspired attacks in Europe and the United States. A growing number of nations are learning that they must be prepared to contend with radicalized youth; home-grown extremists; lone-wolf attackers; and in some cases, returnees from conflicts in such places as Syria and Iraq.[18]

In his testimony, Director Clapper also described the following as among the pervasive and growing threats against the United States and its global national security interests:

> the deteriorating internal security posture in Iraq[;] . . . the growth of foreign cyber capabilities; the proliferation of weapons of mass destruction; aggressive nation-state intelligence efforts against us; an assertive Russia; a competitive China; a dangerous, unpredictable North Korea; a challenging Iran . . . ; lingering ethnic divisions in the Balkans; perpetual conflict and extremism in Africa . . . ; violent political struggles in, among others, the Ukraine, Burma, Thailand and Bangladesh; the specter of mass atrocities; the increasing stress of burgeoning populations; the urgent demands for energy, water and food; the increasing sophistication of transnational crime; the tragedy and magnitude of human trafficking; the

---

[16] Karen K. Myers and Kamyab Sadaghiani, "Millennials in the Workplace: A Communication Perspective on Millennials' Organizational Relationships and Performance," *Journal of Business and Psychology*, Vol. 25, No. 2, June 2010.

[17] James R. Clapper, "Current and Projected Security Threats Against the United States," testimony before the Select Committee on Intelligence, U.S. Senate, Washington D.C., January 29, 2014.

[18] Clapper, 2014.

insidious rot of inventive, synthetic drugs; the potential for pandemic disease occasioned by the growth of drug-resistant bacteria.[19]

At the same time, rates of development of new technologies and improvements, advancements, and cost reduction in existing technologies continue to increase. The quality and accessibility of information continue to improve on a global scale. Moreover, IT

> is entering the big data era. Process power and data storage are becoming almost free; networks and the cloud will provide global access and pervasive services; social media and cybersecurity will be large new markets. . . . This growth and diffusion will present significant challenges for governments and societies, which must find ways to capture the benefits of new IT technologies while dealing with the new threats that those technologies present.[20]

The implications of this changing environment are that the IC needs a workforce with diverse skills and interests to help combat this multitude of complex threats and that this workforce must be able to leverage intelligence from partners and sources around the world from which the information originates and must be able to communicate finished intelligence assessments to warfighters and policymakers to inform decisions.

## Four Groups of Millennials

In the face of these ever-diversifying threats, the increasingly rapid pace of technological change, and the widespread ubiquity of information, the IC will continue its efforts to remain "focused on the missions of cyber intelligence, counterterrorism, counterproliferation, counterintelligence, and on the threats posed by state and nonstate actors challenging U.S. national security and interests worldwide."[21] In doing so however, the IC must also accept the realities of generational change. Generations face and solve problems in different ways; communicate differently; interact differently; and have different expectations about life, work, and personal and professional goals.

Millennials are the largest living generation in the United States and will increasingly occupy positions of influence and responsibility.[22] The more than 73 million

---

[19] Clapper, 2014.

[20] National Intelligence Council, *Global Trends 2030: Alternative Worlds*, Washington, D.C., December 2012, p. 83.

[21] Director of National Intelligence, *The National Intelligence Strategy of the United States of America*, Washington, D.C., 2014.

[22] Richard Fry, "Millennials Overtake Baby Boomers as America's Largest Generation," Pew Research Center website, April 25, 2016.

young adult Americans currently aged 18 to 34 are a majority, though not the entirety, of the generation.[23] Millennials will continue to come of age and enter spheres of influence in which their generational characteristics and outlook may directly or indirectly affect the IC. Among the distinctions millennials have are self-confidence, a desire for self-expression, a liberal nature, an upbeat outlook on life, technological savviness, and an innate openness to change.[24]

This report focuses specifically on the millennials with whom the IC will directly or indirectly have purposeful or meaningful contact. For ease of discussion, we have divided the millennials with whom the IC must be prepared to interact into four principal groups (Figure 1.2). In subsequent chapters, we will describe the relationships among these groups and the perceptions they share, highlight considerations and issues of concern, and discuss potential ramifications for the IC of millennial majorities in each group.

Chapter Two discusses millennials who are **members of the public** and provides background and commentary on their perceptions and how they affect intelligence. This is the largest of our four groups and one of the two most influential. The public, both in the United States and in foreign countries, provides the collective opinion and values that affect societal and governmental change. Public commentary and ardor over public or leaked information about the IC may support or impede its operations and programs. The opinions of members of the public, voiced either through the media or through grassroots communication, influence legislation, regulation, and partnerships that hamper or advance IC budgets, resources, and operations. Federal, state, local, and tribal officials who are not direct customers of the IC's production but who interact with, regulate, oversee, or comment on the IC's work or resources fall into this group.

**Figure 1.2**
**Four Groups of Millennials**

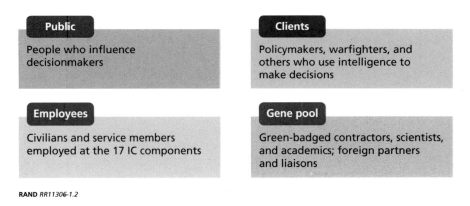

RAND RR11306-1.2

---

[23] U.S. Census Bureau, "American Community Survey: 2009–2013," CB14-219, website, 2014.

[24] Pew Research Center, 2010.

Chapter Three discusses millennials as **clients**, the other of the two most influential groups. The IC will increasingly have to interact with millennials in this group, which includes U.S. decisionmakers, policymakers, warfighters, legislators, and others who directly benefit from and receive intelligence analyses, updates, support and advice. Millennial clients may have informational needs and expectations different from those of their predecessors. Millennials also engage with information in ways different from those of other generations, and this may affect their expectations about how to engage with intelligence. While relating to and communicating with policymakers has long been acknowledged as both a core mission and a sometime weakness of the IC, generational change could complicate the process if the IC does not take steps to understand new client relationships and preferences and adjust its interpersonal communications and technological paradigms to suit.

Chapter Four addresses IC **employees**. Millennials are already working for the IC as civilians and in the military. To maintain a vibrant and productive workforce, IC leaders and managers will have to learn to understand the motivations and influences that inspire and drive millennial employees and the organizational and leadership factors that may be likely to detract from a desire for continued employment. Chapter Four thus addresses the millennial employees' relationship with IC managers and the workplace, discusses opportunities for improving the relationship, and provides some insight on potential issues of concern.

Chapter Five discusses the **IC gene pool**, which consists of millennials the IC finds valuable but who do not, as yet, work for an IC organization. This group includes potential employees the IC may wish to recruit today or in the future and millennial academics, businessmen, contractors, and others whose skills, personal access, or information make them valuable candidates to be sources of information, subject-matter experts, advisors, and outside reviewers on issues of interest to the IC. Domestic and foreign IC business partners fall into this group because they provide continual opportunities for technological, substantive, and qualitative improvement, factors that may increase the depth of the IC gene pool. We have grouped IC contractors, who sometimes move between government and contract employment, with the IC gene pool, although we acknowledge that there is some fuzziness in distinctions between groups.

Figure 1.3 shows some intelligence functions millennials have in each of these groups and illustrates roles that members of more than one group can play.

## Methodology

Our goal was to identify themes about millennials that may affect the ability of intelligence agencies to conduct their missions and to determine whether additional research is warranted. This report does not provide a complete review of all studies, surveys, and literature available about millennials or a comprehensive interviews with IC personnel.

**Figure 1.3**
**Millennials' Roles and Functions in Intelligence**

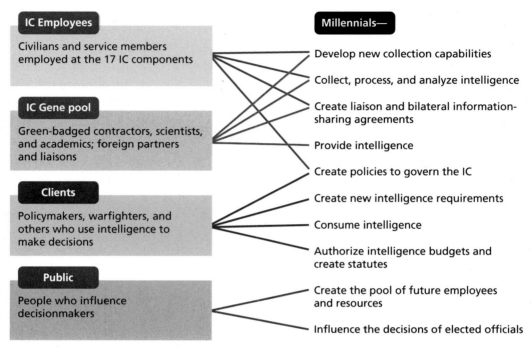

RAND RR11306-1.3

While there is a great deal of popular writing about millennials, it is not necessarily based on rigorous research methodologies. We therefore sought credible sources for all topics we discuss here. Credible research might not have been available for topics we do not address here; in some cases, these areas might offer opportunities for further study. We did not conduct interviews for this project, but many informal discussions informed the background and context, including discussions that occurred at IC and federal government human capital conferences.

As noted earlier, we have defined millennials solely by their birth years for this report and did not study or assess how other demographic affiliations (such as race, ethnicity, religion, gender, sexual orientation, and disability) would affect the generalizations studied in the cited sources. These would obviously affect a person's perspectives and perceptions and thus suggest opportunities for further research. For example, one specific subject it might be helpful to the IC to pursue would be how gender and parenting status affect the views and expectations of millennials. As some millennials are beginning to become parents, new research is emerging on how this workforce has expectations different from those of their nonparent or nonmillennial cohorts for work-life balance, telecommuting, work travel, benefits, and other topics. Given the pace (operational tempo) and travel requirements of many IC career fields, this topic is ripe for further research.

This report focuses on publicly available research and unclassified data from within the IC. We have consistently cited the most current research available at the time of publication, which provided two challenges. New research on millennials is constantly being published, so we anticipate that new studies and surveys will have been released after we completed our research in late 2015. As a result, we anticipate new studies and surveys on millennials emerging after this report is released. Second, because research on millennials is constantly changing, some survey questions that had been asked nearly ten years ago have not been repeated since. We strived always to cite the most recent research, yet we included a small number of older sources, including a survey from 2006 on millennial views on the state of the world, because we found these survey results compelling and relevant and could find no more-recent survey that asked the same questions.

The research reported on here leveraged a series of briefings given by a RAND analyst that sparked heightened the interest of several government offices, but there has been little research on the influence this generation may have on the intelligence and policymaking communities. Areas for scoping potential further research include the changing face of communication, critical thinking, and typical expectations of social interaction.

We believe that the limited research scope for this report, combined with the lack of available research on millennials' perceptions about intelligence and intelligence career fields, warrants further study. These issues will affect the future success of U.S. intelligence missions.

# CHAPTER TWO

# The Public: Perception Is Key

Millennials in the public have collective opinions and values that affect societal and governmental changes. Their commentary and ardor over public or leaked information about the IC may support or impede its operations and programs. Their voice, either through the media or through grassroots communication, can influence legislation and regulation that hampers or advances IC budgets, resources, and operations. Not only American millennials but millennials across the world can affect the U.S. IC in different ways.

Within the United States, millennials influence the decisions and votes of members of Congress and of state, local, and tribal officials on bills and budget authorizations that govern the IC's activities. The perceptions that millennials in the U.S. public have about the IC affect the IC's ability to recruit new employees and influence the private sector's willingness to do business with the IC. Meanwhile, millennials in the foreign public affect the IC's ability to create partnership arrangements and build a pool of potential sources for recruitment.

## U.S. Millennials

Within the U.S. public, millennials affect the IC through their roles in and ability to influence government, media, and the private sector. The opinion that millennials in the U.S. public have of the IC creates its brand and affects its ability to recruit talent, partner in local regions, and do business with the private sector. While Congress has the power to authorize the intelligence budget and create laws, its members are influenced by their constituents, including their millennial constituents.

Outside Congress, millennials are constituents of state, local, and tribal leaders who also have opportunities to affect IC activities. A 2014 incident in Utah illustrates one unanticipated way that these officials can affect the IC's ability to conduct its mission. Lawmakers there were considering a bill to cut off the water supply to a major National Security Agency (NSA) data center that had been proposed in response to the release of classified information about NSA's activities.[1] As *The Salt Lake Tribune* reported, "Committee members expressed some concerns with the bill but no outright opposition."[2] According to Joe Levi, the vice chair of the Davis County Republican Party, "This is not a bill just about a data center, this is a bill about civil rights."[3] This showed that, when debating the bill, Utah lawmakers voiced greater concerns over NSA's surveillance activities than over the effects on national security if this law were passed. Ultimately, this bill was rejected with significantly less fanfare and fewer headlines than when it was proposed.

Outside government, millennials in the United States influence the actions of companies and other organizations, helping determine, for example, whether these companies will partner or cooperate with intelligence agencies. Following recent leaks about specific NSA collection programs, several technology companies began strengthening their encryption and limiting their relationships with the IC. In the next version of the Apple iPhone operating system following the leaks, Apple installed encryption that the company itself cannot break if requested by law enforcement. One headline praised, "Apple's iPhone Encryption Is a Godsend, Even if Cops Hate It."[4]

Whether these changes—the bill in Utah and the new iPhone encryption—were driven by millennials in the U.S. public or by a combination of all generations in the U.S. public, they are in fact driven by public perception that the government has extended its reach too far. Therefore, public perception affects the IC's ability to conduct its mission.

So how do millennials in the U.S. public perceive the IC? Survey data specific to the IC is lacking, but we do know how millennials look at the federal government overall. One author summarizes their perceptions as follows: "We don't blindly trust these institutions; we understand their limitations and know that greed and corruption are inevitable, and thus we are not shocked by scandals and crises."[5] According to the Harvard Institute of Politics, millennials in the United States have trusted the federal government less each year over the past five years; by 2014, only 20 percent of millennials stated that they trusted the federal government.[6] Meanwhile, in a separate survey by the World Economic Forum in 2015, only 11 percent of millennials surveyed agreed

---

[1]   Robert McMillan, "Utah Considers Cutting off Water to the NSA's Monster Data Center," *Wired*, November 20, 2014.

[2]   Nate Carlisle, "Shutting off NSA's Water Gains Support in Utah Legislature," *Salt Lake Tribune*, November 19, 2014.

[3]   Carlisle, 2014.

[4]   Kevin Poulsen, "Apple's iPhone Encryption Is a Godsend, Even if Cops Hate It," *Wired*, October 8, 2014.

[5]   David D. Burstein, *Fast Future: How the Millennial Generation Is Shaping Our World*, Boston: Beacon Press, 2013, p. 6.

[6]   Institute of Politics, "Survey of Young Americans' Attitudes Toward Politics and Public Service," 25th ed., Cambridge, Mass.: Harvard University, April 29, 2014b, p. 18.

with the statement, "I trust the federal government to be honest and fair."[7] Figure 2.1 shows how millennials in the U.S. public trust various institutions.[8]

To communicate with this generation of Americans, the IC needs to do so where millennials are listening. Millennials in the U.S. public have described their primary news sources as being news websites (30 percent of respondents), social media (21 percent), television (18 percent), word of mouth (13 percent), and other (18 percent), yet 66 percent said they were not confident that the news they receive is accurate.[9] Millennials may get much of their information about the IC from traditional media (news websites and television) but have very little trust in these media.[10] Like good analysts, millennials do not trust everything they hear. David Burstein has written that "[t]here can be no doubt that we now have more untrustworthy new sources than we have ever had before, as well as more sources whose trustworthiness is ambiguous."[11] Burstein explained that millennials know that information sources cannot automati-

**Figure 2.1**
**U.S. Millennials' Trust in Several Institutions**

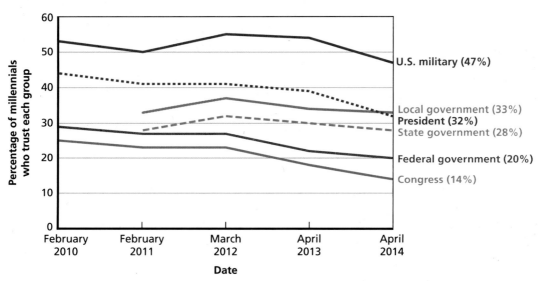

SOURCE: Data from Institute of Politics, "Trust in Institutions and the Political Process," web page, Cambridge, Mass.: Harvard University, 2014a.
NOTE: Percentages in parentheses are the 2014 data.
RAND RR11306-2.1

---

7   World Economic Forum, "Survey Results 2015: Global Shapers Community," 2015, p. 8.

8   Institute of Politics, 2014b, pp. 17–18.

9   "Millennials and News, Fact-Checked," YPulse website, May 29, 2013.

10   Kellie Ryan, "Lessons from the Survey: Millennials Grow More Partisan, Think Washington Is Broken," Cambridge, Mass.: Institute of Politics, Harvard University, May 7, 2013.

11   Burstein, 2013, p. 63.

cally be trusted and have grown up learning to always check and recheck their information. Therefore, it would be important for the IC to communicate its messages without discrepancies or other signs that IC analytic content may be untrustworthy.

Edward Snowden has provided a type of litmus test for public perception: Those who believe the documents he released are truthful may be divided on whether he was justified in his actions because the secrets he revealed should be in the public domain or whether he was not justified because he jeopardized national security. For example, when a Harvard Institute of Politics poll asked "whether [millennials] considered Edward Snowden to be more of a patriot or traitor—more than half (52 percent) indicated that they were unsure nearly five months after his story broke."[12] Poll respondents were then asked a hypothetical: "If you found yourself in a position similar to that of Edward Snowden, would you release the classified documents to the media, or would you not release the documents?" Of the millennials who answered, 50 percent were unsure, and 15 percent said they would release the documents. Within this generation, only 22 percent are sure that Edward Snowden jeopardized national security with his actions. (See Figure 2.2.)

What if the question is posed differently, to ask about specific programs? The Pew Research Center did so, asking about the CIA's interrogation program: "Young people [age 18–29] are divided over the CIA's post-9/11 methods: 44 percent of those under 30 say they were justified while 36 percent disagree. Among those 50 and older, most

**Figure 2.2**
**Millennials' Perceptions of Edward Snowden**

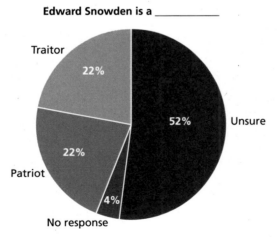

SOURCE: Data from Institute of Politics, 2014b, p. 11.
RAND RR1306-2.2

---

[12] Institute of Politics, "While Edward Snowden's Legacy May Be An Open Question Among Millennials, Collecting Personal Information for National Security Is Not," Cambridge, Mass.: Harvard University, undated.

(60%) think the methods were justified."[13] Older Americans are thus more likely to support the CIA's interrogation program than millennials.

But despite this mistrust of and uncertainty about the IC, millennials in the U.S. public believe that government has both the responsibility and the ability to respond to war, terrorism, social unrest, cyber security, and political instability.[14] It may seem counterintuitive that millennials do not trust the government yet simultaneously believe that only the government is positioned to respond to these threats. This dichotomy creates an opportunity for the IC to demonstrate its ability to meet the country's security challenges. Who else, besides the IC, is positioned to identify and mitigate these threats?

The IC can increase the public's understanding of its missions by increasing the frequency and depth of discussions in open forums. By communicating in forums where millennials are listening, the IC can explain its missions and what it does to accomplish those missions. Discussions of capabilities and the value they provide create a shared understanding and possibly some agreement that these capabilities are vital to national defense.

Within specific missions and capabilities, intelligence agencies could provide clearer job descriptions of and explanations for the roles of government employees. For example, at each agency, what is the difference between the roles of *collector* and *analyst*? What are the core job functions at NSA? What type of collection does the CIA conduct, and how does this differ from what NSA and the National Geospatial-Intelligence Agency do? How do the roles of analysts vary across agencies? How do intelligence officers at the Federal Bureau of Investigation contribute to law enforcement and criminal prosecutions? How does the Department of Homeland Security use intelligence to strengthen America's borders and to interdict drugs and human smuggling? Raising millennials' awareness about the work fellow citizens do for intelligence agencies can remove the stigma and mystery that some Americans associate with working in intelligence. This could both raise the IC brand and facilitate recruiting activities.

Prior to the Snowden leaks, most millennials received their information about the IC from TV shows, movies, and other popular culture. Hollywood's depictions of intelligence are designed to be dramatic, not accurate, allowing studios to create stories in which intelligence agencies are all knowing, ever watching, and capable of many fantastical capabilities. In contrast, the Department of Defense has worked for decades with film studios to create, with varying levels of success, realistic depictions of life in the military to clear up inconsistencies. The studios benefit from access to aircraft carriers, fighter jets, and other exclusive settings, while the department gains influence over the script and relevant details. Providing accurate depictions of life in the military

---

[13] Pew Research Center, "About Half See CIA Interrogation Methods as Justified," web page, December 15, 2014b.

[14] Deloitte, 2014.

has aided recruiting efforts and influenced public opinion. Intelligence agencies on the other hand, remain mostly closed to extensive cooperation with Hollywood. In the few instances in which IC media relations offices have worked with television and movie producers, they did so agency by agency. Because policies, practices, and agency cultures are so different from one agency to the next, messages about agency missions, focus, and capabilities are often inconsistent and confusing to the public.

A related opportunity for the IC to engage millennials is helping them understand IC budget and portfolio decisions and how these connect with capabilities. The goal would be to help the American public understand why intelligence budgets are so large and what resources are spent on, but without providing sensitive details within specific programs. When the Director of National Intelligence released the value of the National Intelligence Program budget request in 2007, it was the first time intelligence budget data had been declassified. The IC could provide additional details to explain what portions of that budget were spent on satellites, human capital, and workforce development and address similar topics to provide transparency into the types of activities that occur in the IC.

## Foreign Millennials

American and foreign millennials are different both because they have grown up in different countries and cultures, with different values, education, and economic opportunities, and because the IC needs different things from each. Millennials in the foreign public may be either U.S. allies or adversaries, and individuals in the same country can be either. As allies, millennials may influence a government's intelligence-sharing relationship with the United States; as adversaries, millennials may affect the ability of the United States to collect intelligence. For both allies and adversaries, the United States wants to build its network of sources and liaisons through both official and unofficial intelligence-sharing channels. The perceptions that millennials in these countries have about the United States and U.S. intelligence can influence their willingness to share information and the type of information they will share. These perceptions may, alternatively, inspire foreign millennials to use denial and deception techniques against U.S. collection and analysis.

The characteristics of millennials are different across regions and countries. In some countries, government censorship limits access to information, replacing transparency with propaganda designed to serve regime goals. Because they are unable to draw unbiased conclusions, millennials in these countries may have very different perceptions about their own country's power and the actions of the United States. Some countries' economic realities parallel those in the United States, such as creating job markets for educated youths. But in others, especially in the Middle East, youth unemployment is severe, creating an entire generation that relies on government subsidies and lacks work experience.

As another example, millennials everywhere have always lived in a world in which NATO exists and in which Russia is more of a nonkinetic threat than a nuclear threat. This generation barely remembers—for those who were even born then—the fall of the Berlin Wall and the collapse of the Soviet Union. Therefore, millennials of any country may be less convinced than other generations of the value of NATO and its mission.

This section provides a brief world tour of millennials across continents, highlighting topics that may affect how these populations perceive U.S. intelligence partnerships. Additional local factors, such as ethnic or religious tensions and domestic spying, would likely influence millennials' perspectives in each region and should be studied further to inform IC outreach decisions in each country.

### Asia

By 2020, more than 60 percent of the world's millennials will live in Asia. In these countries, many millennials "are better educated and have higher earning power than older generations."[15] Within Asia, the two largest populations of millennials are in China, with 382 million, and India, with 306 million.[16] The millennial populations of these two countries alone are each comparable with the entire population of all Americans of all ages. But most significant for the IC, this generation of Asians shares one key attribute with its American counterparts. These millennials want to see corporations partner with government to accomplish big goals:

> More than 86% of millennials surveyed in Mainland China, Hong Kong, India, Japan, and Singapore expect businesses to be actively involved in solving important issues such as economy, environment and healthcare; in China, the world's largest population of millennials, as much as 92% of millennials demand business involvement. The increasing involvement of businesses with social issues is seen as a key factor for success.[17]

Yet optimism among millennials is not consistent from one Asian country to the next. Japanese millennials are "the least optimistic globally"; "over 70% do not feel they can make a positive impact on the world."[18] For governments to partner with the IC, their members must believe that their countries will be better off for this relationship. Since perceptions and optimism vary across countries, including in Asia, the IC

---

[15] Craig Briggs and Kathryn Sloane, "What Do Asia's Millennials See Ahead?" *Marketing Daily*, August 20, 2013.

[16] MSLGroup, "Asian Millennials Expect Business to Solve Important Social Issues and Empower Gen Y to Drive Change Together," web page, September 17, 2014.

[17] MSLGroup, 2014.

[18] MSLGroup, 2014.

will need to take a different, nuanced approach to engaging with millennials and motivating them to partner with the United States.

### Latin America

The challenges millennials in Latin America perceive are distinctly different from those their Asian and U.S. counterparts perceive: "Latin Millennials see corruption and a lagging education system as enormous barriers to growth and success, with 75 percent ranking corruption as the top issue hindering their country's growth, followed by the education system (51 percent) and political leadership (42 percent)."[19] Yet despite these obstacles, Latin American millennials are among the most optimistic, with 72 percent believing that their countries' best days are ahead, and 82 percent believing that they can make a local difference (see Figure 2.3).[20]

One millennial who made a local difference was Colombian Oscar Morales. In 2008, he successfully organized Colombian millennials to pressure the Revolutionary Armed Forces of Colombia (FARC) into releasing hostages by creating a Facebook page called "One Million Voices Against FARC." Within a week, he had 100,000 followers, and he planned a protest demanding the release of hundreds of hostages, including

**Figure 2.3**
**Millennials' Beliefs—Whether They Can Make a Difference**

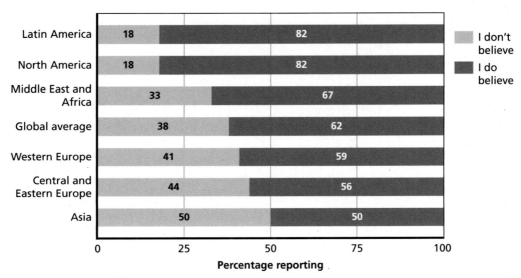

SOURCE: Data from Telefónica, 2013a, p. 42.
**RAND** *RR11306-2.3*

---

[19] Teresa Meek, "Global Survey: Today's Millennials Are Tech-Savvy, Footloose, Confident and Practical," Coca-Cola Journey website, October 13, 2014.

[20] Telefónica, "Telefónica Global Millennial Survey: Focus on Global," fact sheet, undated.; Telefónica, 2013a, p. 42.

a prominent politician, her campaign manager, and the baby her campaign manager gave birth to in confinement. Within a few days of the protest, the new mother, baby, and a third hostage were released. One month later, Morales organized an even larger protest, with more than 100,000 people. The momentum he created ultimately led to a successful rescue mission later that summer.[21] Millennials who believe they can make a difference have opportunities to leverage technology, such as social media, to build momentum for their causes.

Latin American millennials are more optimistic for their countries' futures than their peers elsewhere (see Figure 2.3); as a result, they may look for benefits different from those millennials in other regions look for when considering partnerships with the United States. The IC can consider how a partnership with the United States will benefit each country's populace on issues that matter to this age group, then tailor its approach and messaging to these benefits.

## Middle East and Africa

Millennials in the Middle East and Africa list the two most important issues their countries face as terrorism and political unrest, respectively.[22] Coincidentally, both are priority topics in the IC, providing an alignment between the goals of millennials in these countries and the IC.

The Middle East has an enormous population of millennials and very high youth unemployment rates. According to Juan Cole, a professor at the University of Michigan, millennials consist of over one-third of the world's 400 million Arabs. This is a generation that is generally better educated than their parents. In 1980, only about one-half of the citizens of Arabic-speaking countries could read and write. In 2000, the literacy rate for 15-to-24-year-olds was around 80 percent, and in three countries— Tunisia, Libya, and Bahrain—it was over 90 percent.

Literacy is significant because millennials in the Middle East and Africa own smartphones at rates higher than those in North America, Latin America, and Central and Eastern Europe (see Figure 2.4), and literacy provides them the skills to connect outside their borders in ways that previous generations were never able to. In Egypt, higher literacy rates led to a rise in the number of newspapers that, "despite the country's censorship regime, often demonstrated a streak of independence."[23] Literacy provides this generation with the ability to learn from, communicate with, and organize with peers outside their own villages.

In Iran, where 70 percent of the population is under 30, 4.5 million students were in universities in 2014, providing a surplus of highly educated, liberal-minded men and

---

[21] Burstein, 2013; David D. Burstein, "Innovation Agents: Oscar Morales and One Million Voices Against FARC," *Fast Company*, May 21, 2012.

[22] Telefónica, "Middle East & Africa: What Makes Millennials Tick?" November 28, 2013b.

[23] Cole, 2014, p. 14.

**Figure 2.4**
**Global Millennials Who Report Owning a Smartphone, Laptop, Desktop, or Tablet**

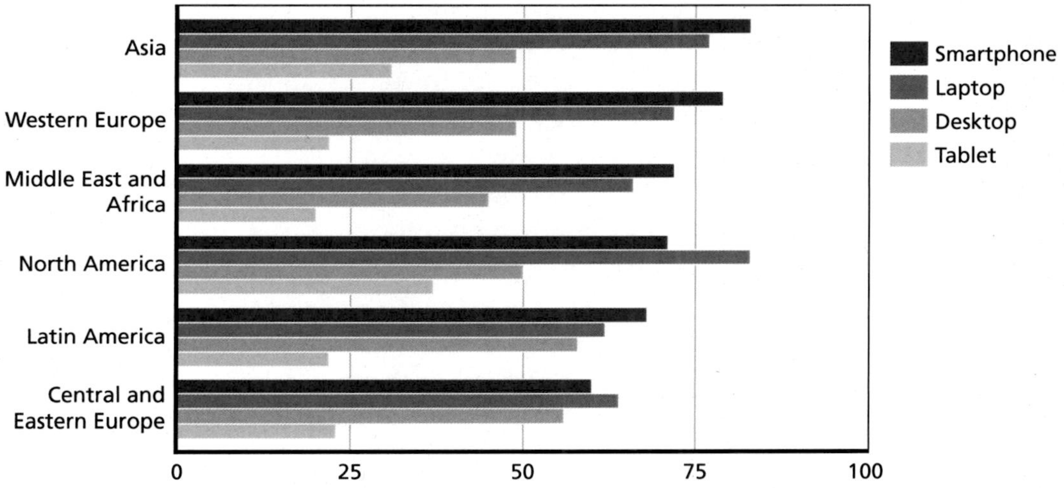

SOURCE: Data from Telefónica, 2013a, p 7.
RAND RR11306-2.4

women.[24] When millennials in Iran have the economic means to leave, they do, result-ing in a brain drain to Europe for jobs and other benefits.

## Europe

Millennials in Europe face a different environment from the ones their counterparts in Latin America, Asia, and the United States face, where economic realities are improv-ing. While younger generations are overtaking the sizes of older generations on most continents, Europe stands out as a region in which 47 percent of the population was over the age of 50 in 2015.[25] Comparatively, in the United States, only 33 percent of the population was over 50 in 2012.[26] While American millennials may have seen positive signs indicating the end of the economic recession—such as finding jobs and new opportunities—European millennials remain in recessed economies. Yet, like millennials on other continents, the perceptions of those in Europe vary across coun-tries. Some European millennials, such as those in Germany and the United Kingdom (UK), are significantly more satisfied with progress in their countries than millennials are in Italy, Spain, and Greece.[27] (See Figure 2.5.)

---

[24] Burstein, 2013; Afshin Rohani, "A State of Unrest: Iran's Youth Face Unemployment and Rising Apathy," *Urban Times*, June 19, 2014.

[25] Bruce Stokes, "Who Are Europe's Millennials?" Washington, D.C.: Pew Research Center, February 9, 2015.

[26] U.S. Census Bureau, "Table 1. Population by Age and Sex: 2012," *Age and Sex Composition in the United States*, 2012.

[27] Stokes, 2015.

**Figure 2.5**
**European Millennials' Satisfaction with Their Country's Direction, Compared with Older Generations**

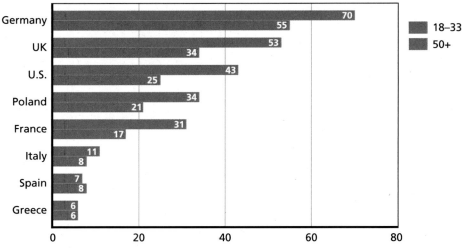

**Percentage satisfied with the way things are going in their country**

SOURCE: Stokes, 2015. Data taken from spring 2014 Pew Global Attitudes survey. Used with permission.
RAND RR11306-2.5

In terms of their goals and priorities, millennials in Europe believe that "eliminating poverty is one of the most important ways to make a difference in the world."[28] Compare this to millennials in the Middle East and Africa, who believe that terrorism and political unrest are the most important issues, and it becomes clear that millennials' priorities are shaped by their local environment.

In Russia, millennials have been shaped by the fall of the Soviet Union and rise of Vladimir Putin:

> According to the Levada Center, an independent polling organization in Moscow, Putin's high approval rating among young people tops even his numbers among an older generation that remembers the days of empire and views Crimea—and even Ukraine—as essentially Russian.
>
> Eighteen-to-24-year-olds—the youngest group among 1,600 people surveyed in late May—backed Putin more than any other age bracket, at 86 percent, said Karina Pipiya, a spokeswoman for the polling center. Eighty-two percent of Russians ages 40 to 54 said they supported Putin, she said.[29]

---

[28] Telefónica, "European Millennials," *Telefónica Global Millennial Survey*, 2014.

[29] Abigail Hauslohner, "Young Russians Never Knew the Soviet Union, but They Hope to Recapture Days of Its Empire," *Washington Post*, June 10, 2014.

Putin's high approval numbers have been attributed to nostalgia for a powerful Soviet world power that no longer exists and state-sponsored propaganda campaigns that falsify school textbooks and news reports. Yet some millennials protest Putin's oppressive acts, and their cause is symbolized by a well-known punk music group called Pussy Riot.[30]

Around the world, millennials generally have more access to information and higher education than their parents had. Their personal views may be more accessible to the IC as they continuously access and post to social media sites. But how millennials apply the benefits of information and education—whether they flee to better economies or stay and improve their homelands—depends on their self-interests and beliefs in whether they can make a difference. From one country to another, millennials process information differently and have different goals. The IC has the same ability to influence its own brand and perceptions internationally that it does in the United States, but one size does not fit all. The IC's ability to connect with millennials in the foreign public will affect its allied and adversarial relationships, information sharing, and collection and analysis capabilities.

---

[30] Brendan Kent, "Millennial Must-Read: Defining Pussy Riot," Cambridge, Mass.: Institute of Politics, Harvard University, 2014.

# CHAPTER THREE

# Millennial Clients: Policymakers and Decisionmakers for Decades to Come

*Clients* are the decision- and policymakers, warfighting commanders, legislators, and others who directly benefit from and receive intelligence analyses, updates, support, and advice from the IC. Clients continuously levy intelligence requirements on the community and often pose difficult and time-sensitive questions to IC member agencies. They may expect to receive continuous intelligence support and are likely to rely on IC assistance in conducting their own professional duties. The President of the United States and the cabinet secretaries are clients, relying on the IC for daily strategic-level support to decisionmaking and ongoing long-term support for policymaking. Deployed service members; state, local, and tribal law enforcement agencies; homeland security officials; and agents of numerous other government entities rely on intelligence information for targeting, planning, case development, force protection, and operational and tactical decisionmaking. Millennials are beginning to fill positions in all these roles and will continue moving up through ranks of government as their careers progress.

Relating to and communicating with policymakers have long been acknowledged as both core missions and sometime weaknesses of the IC. Client reliance on IC support for decisionmaking may vary broadly from individual to individual, and relationships between the IC and individual policymakers may likewise vary accordingly. However, over time, the IC has developed routines and normalized information flows for the vast majority of its clients. Generational change could complicate these relationships and communication processes unless the IC takes steps to understand its new clients and to explore new preferences for adjustments in interpersonal communications and technological paradigms. Policymakers in any generation may vary in the way they prefer to receive information, in the ways in which they process and use information, and in the relationship(s) that they have with information stakeholders. Millennials are no exception.

## How Millennials Process and Use Information

Millennial clients of the IC will have grown up connected to information through technology that is available 24/7. They may bring that preference for continuous reporting to their roles as decision- and policymakers (see Figure 3.1). Pew research suggests that millennials "treat their multi-tasking hand-held gadgets almost like a body part—for better and worse. More than eight-in-ten say they sleep with a cell phone glowing by the bed."[1] Unlike policymakers of earlier generations, whose bedside phone was a symbol of their professionalism and willingness to handle crises 24 hours a day, as required, millennials actually use their phones throughout the night, to "disgorge texts, phone calls, emails, songs, news, videos, games and wake-up jingles."[2]

The IC historically provides intelligence to most policymakers in early morning face-to-face book briefings five days a week, in afternoon updates, and as needed when new or critical information becomes available. Yet by the time millennials get out of bed in the morning, they may already be up to speed on overnight events on their topics of interest and may not appreciate it if their morning intelligence briefing contains intelligence that is eight hours old. Further, millennials may prefer continuous reporting and routine direct access to intelligence and intelligence experts and may have specific preferences for the manner in and style with which information is

**Figure 3.1**
**Percentage of Americans Who Sleep with a Cell Phone on or Next to the Bed**

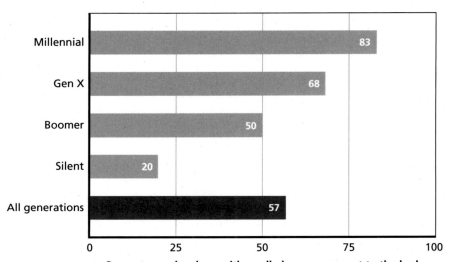

SOURCE: Pew Research Center, 2010, p. 6. Used with permission.
RAND RR11306-3.1

---

[1]  Pew Research Center, 2010.

[2]  Pew Research Center, 2010.

made available, shared, and used. Millennials are "digital natives"—tending to choose texting over phone calls; emails over face-to-face meetings; and online, self-directed, flexible access to information over traditional briefing charts filled with blocks of text. Their preference for receiving intelligence from people they trust in their social network may affect how they build trust in their intelligence briefers, whom they want to receive intelligence from, and how they wish to receive it.

Millennial clients who receive continuous updates on issues of importance to them may find that the IC provides too little, too late in a routine morning briefing or occasional crisis-related update. They may find their preferred digital news aggregator and crowd-sourced flow of information to be timelier and more accessible. Because of their communications preferences, millennial policymakers may be increasingly likely to want an ongoing electronic dialogue with their intelligence interlocutors, rather than an update book or a response memo, something that most IC agencies are not structured or resourced to provide.

Additionally, the IC has, for decades, had to contend with the agenda-setting effects of conventional media, spending much of its time and energy attempting to provide classified updates to policymakers on unclassified breaking news stories. Still, the IC has, arguably, been capable of following all major media streams and preparing accordingly. In the face of nearly unlimited sources of information and near daily instances of stories going "viral" on waves of social media attention, the IC will have to know more than the collective wisdom of the Internet and will need to find new ways of gaining and keeping the attention of policymakers. As the average human attention span continues to decrease, especially among those living a digital lifestyle,[3] keeping the attention of policymakers may be increasingly difficult.

## Millennial Analyst-Policy Relationships

Much has been written about the natural tensions between analysts and policymakers. Policymakers rely on analysts for estimative judgments on a wide range of issues but are often critical of what they perceive as analysts' inability to provide adequate intelligence on issues that are central to particular policy agendas. Analysts work hard to provide expert judgments to support policymaker needs but are professionally admonished against, if not prohibited from, entering into discussions that border on policy criticism or creation.[4] Generational change may alter that paradigm as well. Millennials value teamwork and are accustomed to collaboration. They have a tendency to share

---

[3]  A 2015 Microsoft study defined a *digital lifestyle* as one led by "those who consume more media, are multi-screeners, social media enthusiasts, or earlier adopters of technology" (Microsoft Canada, "Attention Spans: Consumer Insights," Spring 2015, p. 24).

[4]  Jack Davis, "Tensions in Analyst-Policymaker Relations: Opinions, Facts, and Evidence," The Sherman Kent Center for Intelligence Analysis, CIA website, January 2003.

information rapidly within their networks and to expect others to share accordingly. They also self-report as being team oriented and wanting to make a difference in the world.[5]

While intelligence analysts of the past have been very careful not to cross the line into policymaking, increasing requests for "opportunity analysis" over the past decade have begun to blur the line for many analysts. Today, many IC agencies craft "analytic lines," the official analytic position of an IC entity on a particular topic, and consider all requests from policymakers on that topic in light of the agency's official position.

In the future, both the millennial policymaker and the millennial intelligence officer may see themselves more as members of the same larger team, sharing information continuously and advancing policy in support of U.S. national security interests. This policymaker-intelligence officer teamwork may outpace IC agencies' abilities to formally adjust analytic lines and may require new paradigms for quality assurance on intelligence analysis and dissemination.

---

[5] Pew Research Center, 2010.

# CHAPTER FOUR

# Intelligence Community Employees: The Intelligence Workforce

A growing number of current IC employees were born after 1980. Millennials are civilians, active-duty service members, and reservists. Much has been discussed, debated, and inferred about this generation of spies, but little has been studied, documented, and analyzed. The employment cycle of a millennial in the IC will, on the surface, look identical to that of any previous generation—hiring, onboarding, developing, and retaining—but the expectations these employees have for their careers differ greatly from those of previous generations. See Box 1.

Will the millennial generation perceive the IC to be a desirable employer? Will millennial intelligence officers desire a revolving-door employment path, one that lets them join and leave the IC easily? What distinct skills can millennials bring to the IC, and how will agencies invest in or inhibit the development of their skills?

At every stage in the employment cycle, millennials present opportunities for agencies to diversify their talent base, incorporate new skills, and introduce new perspectives, while simultaneously creating new challenges in keeping these workers engaged and motivated amid the bureaucracy. Like other workers, millennials will

---

**Box 1**
**Questions for IC Leaders**

**Hiring**
Do the IC's current policies and practices artificially narrow the pool of millennial candidates?

**Onboarding**
How do initial experiences affect employment engagement and longevity in the IC?

**Developing Skills**
How do millennials absorb learning and knowledge, and does this align with how the IC provides learning and knowledge?

**Retaining Talent**
How do millennials plan their career paths, and do intelligence career fields align with these goals?

---

take pride in their work, value their professional contributions, and seek career opportunities that align with certain goals. Yet more than other generations, these goals will include personal goals, including work-life balance; millennials may therefore not follow traditional career paths.

Public service matters to millennials, yet they may be less inclined to trust government, the IC, and the military than their elders were. Millennials already employed by IC agencies or in the hiring process have self-selected this career path and, therefore, are generally more confident in the IC's missions than are other millennials. When we were conducting briefings on our research, some current leaders and managers across IC agencies suggested that the IC does not need to convince anyone to come work for it. Yet needs remain unfulfilled in critical career fields—especially within cyber and science, technology, engineering, and mathematics (STEM) fields and in critical language skills—across agencies. The ability of the IC to attract the talent it needs will continue to challenge agencies as more experienced employees retire and as the skills needed for the future cannot be found within agencies' current cadres. Further, the desire of millennials to move between jobs[1]—including between the public and private sectors—means that agencies will need robust midcareer hiring mechanisms to reattract, rehire, and continue to develop millennials for decades to come.

## Hiring Dilemmas

The millennial applicant probably meets many of the IC's skill and education requirements. This is the most educated generation in American history, and its diversity provides openness to working with different types of people who can bring different perspectives to a problem or project. Thanks to shifting demographics, immigration from various regions, and retention of cultural identities, these future employees have a deeper understanding of the regions and cultures they will be analyzing than many of their more-experienced colleagues do.[2] They may speak or understand foreign languages, such as Vietnamese, Persian, and Twi.[3] Because of military service, education abroad, and overseas family ties, they often understand that the behaviors and actions considered "normal" in the United States may have different meanings in different contexts elsewhere. This is knowledge that cannot be taught in textbooks, and it provides millennials in intelligence analysis and collection roles with an intuitive understanding of mirror-imaging and other common biases.

---

[1]   PricewaterhouseCoopers, "Millennials at Work: Reshaping the Workplace," New York, 2011, p. 7.

[2]   Pew Research Center, 2010, p. 10.

[3]   Of adults aged 18–34, 25 percent speak a language other than English at home today, as opposed to 11 percent in 1980 (U.S. Census Bureau, "Language Other than English Spoken at Home, Age 18 to 34," graphic, undated). This does not include millennials who speak only English at home but use other languages outside the home, e.g., heritage speakers who use English with cohabitants because it is the only shared language.

Many of the benefits of hiring millennials become challenges within the IC's current hiring process: This pool of applicants may be harder to clear than ever before. Their vast overseas experience may provide critical language skills and foreign cultural awareness but may also complicate or impede the security clearance process.

When hiring for deployable positions, hiring managers will be pleased to hear that "millennials have a strong appetite for working overseas and 71 percent expect and want to do an overseas assignment during their career." Many millennials expect to travel for work and want to use their careers to see the world; however, they may have narrow expectations for that travel, specifically the ability to choose locations they perceive as desirable. They rank their top work destinations as the UK and Australia, and "only 11% were willing to work in India and 2% in mainland China. Despite this, over half said they would be willing to work in a less developed country to further their career."[4] As a result, hardship positions—those in challenging, distant, or dangerous places—may continue to be difficult to fill.

This generation has come of age during an economic downturn. Its members have an average of $45,000 of debt,[5] which is more student and personal debt than previous generations had at their ages. While this leads to a desire for reliable employment, which is good for intelligence agencies, it also leads to a desire for higher salaries, which may put agencies at competitive disadvantages with private-sector employers. Millennials' debts create obstacles for security clearances, yet these workers are generally more careful with their finances than older generations,[6] making them less risky from a security clearance perspective. They tend not to rack up credit card debt as much as older generations, and they are generally buying homes later in life.[7]

Historically, the military has been a ripe training ground for future civilian intelligence officers, with military service providing an understanding of intelligence capabilities and providing the skills agencies desire. Yet the military's prohibitions on tattoos and body piercings relegate a large pool of the millennial population as ineligible for service. More than one-third of millennials have tattoos; about half of those have between two and five tattoos; and 18 percent have six or more. Restrictions vary by military service, but tattoos are generally prohibited outright on the face, neck, hands, and wrists. Additional individual service restrictions include requirements to document tattoos annually, prohibition of "sleeve" tattoos, prohibition of four or more

---

[4]  PricewaterhouseCoopers, 2011, p. 5.

[5]  PNC, "PNC Financial Independence Survey—Part II A National Study of the Financial Behaviors of 20-Somethings," March 2012.

[6]  "Think You Know the Next Gen Investor?" *UBS Investor Watch*, January 2014, p 7.

[7]  Pew Research Center, 2010.

tattoos below the knee or elbow, prohibition for enlisted members with some existing tattoos to apply for a commission, and limitations on size and subject matter.[8]

Additionally, one-quarter of millennials have a piercing somewhere other than an earlobe, which, if on a visible location of the body (tongue, nose, lips, face, etc.) would make them ineligible for military service.[9] As tattoos and piercings continue to grow in popularity as a lifestyle choice, intelligence components of the military services may find their pools of eligible candidates shrinking. Will the military of the future have to adjust its definition of "sensible" earrings to expand its candidate pool?

The recent legalization of marijuana in several states aligns with the position of the 69 percent of millennials who believe marijuana should be legal.[10] Will the IC exclude millennial recruits based on their use of marijuana, even for recruits with specialized STEM or language skills?

The IC will face a decision to either hire the best talent in the market or to hire only from the subset of the population that has little international experience; no debt; and, for military intelligence, no disallowed piercings or tattoos. Candidates will have to toe the federal line on substance use, even if they have grown up in states where legalized marijuana has become a cultural norm. Then, the IC must convince individuals that it is a better employer than the private sector, where they are not required to give up their piercings, hide their tattoos, or abstain from marijuana and are not prevented from personal travel to certain countries. While government employment still offers financial benefits comparable to those in the private sector,[11] the wait for a clearance and the burdens of employment may be a disincentive to application for many potential employees or recruits.

## A Tale of Two Onboardings

Imagine the first day of a new job. The new employee gets to the office, is greeted at the front door by her new manager, and is immediately shown to her new office. Her access passes are made as soon as she walks in the door. Her computer is already set up, and her platform preference—PC versus Apple—has been asked for and accom-

---

[8]  For specific service regulations on tattoos, mutilations, and body piercings, see Army Regulation 670-1, *Wear and Appearance of Army Uniforms and Insignia*,"April 10, 2015, p. 10; Navy Administrative Instruction 110/06 (amplifies Navy's policy on tattoos, body art, brands, mutilations, and dental ornamentation), October 1, 2003; Air Force Instruction 36-2903, *Dress and Personal Appearance of Air Force Personnel*, July 18, 2011, p. 22; and Marine Admin Message 198/07, "Amplification to the Marine Corps Tattoo Policy," January 15, 2010.

[9]  Pew Research Center, 2010, p. 57.

[10]  Pew Research Center, "Generations and Issues," in Pew Research Center, *Millennials in Adulthood: Detached from Institutions, Networked with Friends*, March 7, 2014a.

[11]  Congressional Budget Office, "Comparing the Compensation of Federal and Private-Sector Employees," Washington, D.C., Pub. No. 4403, January 2012.

modated in advance. An information technology representative is there to help set up passwords, explain the different corporate accounts, and set up phone and voicemail. The new employee meets with human resources to go over benefits, nondisclosure agreements, required training, and payroll information. Facility specialists give her a tour of the building and hand her the company mug and jacket. She then has meetings with her new coworkers and manager. Other new hires from all sections of the company gather together that afternoon for an orientation to company culture, presented by a senior employee who volunteered for the responsibility. The next day, the new employee begins work on her new projects and has lunch with her new team. Various new hire trainings are sprinkled into her schedule in two-day increments over the next six months, allowing her to acclimate to her work environment while applying the new training she learns.

Another new employee starts work today for a different employer. At this location, the new employee waits 30 minutes to be met at the front desk by someone he will never see again, who escorts him to a classroom filled with new hires from different departments and job fields. They each receive a mug and pen with the organization's logo. For the first four to six hours, until his identity badge arrives, he cannot leave the room without an escort. He watches several videos about security policies and procedures and signs legal paperwork. He will receive rote training from briefers who are not invested in their own futures with the organization, much less that of the new employee. He will not meet with his new manager or coworkers and will not receive information about his new job or projects. He has no online access to or connectivity with his future team or projects. Weeks later, he arrives at his new office without an understanding of his new role or how these training sessions fit in with his new responsibilities.

The difference between these scenarios is the difference between an organization that wants its new hires to feel welcome, wanted, and immediately embedded into the team and one that unintentionally sends a message that it finds someone new showing up an inconvenience. Research shows that "86% of new hires decide to stay or leave a company within their first six months and new employees are 69% more likely to stay longer than three years if they experience well-structured onboarding."[12] First impressions matter. An organization that strips new hires of their technology and their connectivity to the outside world and simultaneously imposes travel and lifestyle restrictions should consider the ramifications of alienating employees before they are engaged in the mission.

---

[12] Karie Willyerd, "Social Tools Can Improve Employee Onboarding," *Harvard Business Review*, December 21, 2012.

## Developing Skills

Millennial employees are generally highly educated and value learning new skills,[13] yet their approach to learning may not coincide with an intelligence agency's approaches to teaching. Many are accustomed to self-teaching and collaborating in teams to learn new subjects.

One study suggests that millennials learn best in short bursts, rather than by sitting through lengthy training sessions.[14] Growing up as multitaskers, they are accustomed to interactive stimulation rather than lectures, which may not fit with week-long new-hire orientation programs and other training courses. The millennial employee is happy to collaborate with coworkers, share information, and cross-train in a variety of disciplines.[15] They want the opportunity to grow and learn. What opportunities for career and skill growth does the agency provide? Are employees allowed to self-direct into specialties, or are they required to work only where management has assigned them? How will employees react to constant barriers to information access? Will current rules and structures impede innovation and creativity? How will employers help them grow and keep them productive? Giving instructions and sending them off to work will not be enough.

Communication styles can be a source of friction; many millennials prefer instant messaging, email, and text messages over phone calls and corporate meetings. A senior vice president of human resources at a 7,000-person company asked employees whether they felt informed by management. The baby boomers wanted more information delivered to them by their managers, while the millennials felt well-informed by the company website and did not want additional management discussions.[16]

## Redefining Retention

The average millennial does not expect to remain in one job for an entire career (see Figure 4.1), so intelligence agencies can anticipate their employees having career paths that cross agencies and the private sector. Yet this trend is not specific to millennials, and millennials are hardly the generation with the highest employment attrition:

> Contrary to popular perceptions Millennials actually stay with their employers longer than Generation X workers did at the same ages. This reflects the fact that Millennials face a labor market characterized by longer job tenure, fewer employer

---

[13] Pew Research Center, 2010, p. 41.

[14] Susan Milligan, "Capturing the Wisdom of Four Generations," *HR Magazine*, Vol. 59, No. 11, November 2014.

[15] Milligan, 2014.

[16] Milligan, 2014.

**Figure 4.1**
**Number of Employers Millennials Expect to Work for, Based on Global Survey**

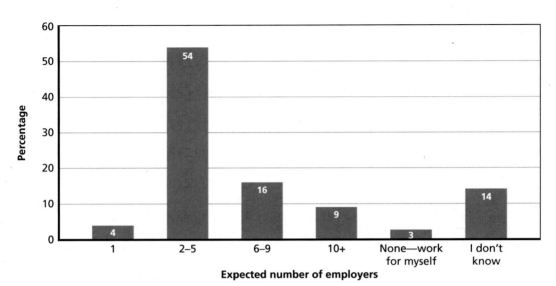

SOURCE: PricewaterhouseCoopers, 2011, p. 7. Used with permission.
RAND *RR11306-4.1*

switches and other types of career transitions, and lower overall fluidity in the labor market. . . . Millennials are less likely to have been with their employer for less than a year than Generation X workers were at the same age, and they are more likely to have been with their employer for a fairly long period like 3 to 6 years.[17]

Varied experiences can provide employees with diverse perspectives and appreciation of the needs of intelligence clients. Yet these career paths require agencies to provide onramps for millennials entering the IC later in their careers or returning after a jaunt elsewhere. Do hiring, retention, and security clearance practices and processes accommodate the future needs of agencies' workforces? Are agency alumni associations designed to keep former employees engaged, and do they provide onramps back into the workforce? And do they leverage connections that current employees may have to their former workplaces?

As millennials consider where to work, they desire employers that reward competency over tenure. Are project assignments, promotions, and salaries aligned with years of experience or performance in the IC?

When intelligence agencies have to compete to keep employees, do they offer benefits and rewards that are competitive with those other employers offer? Almost 50 percent of millennials desire to work from anywhere any time, without being forced into an 8-hour workday; about 25 percent of millennials want to work from home part

---

[17]  Council of Economic Advisors, "15 Economic Facts About Millennials," Washington, D.C., Executive Office of the President, October 2014, p. 29.

of the time; and 14 percent of millennials do not take a car to work (see Box 2). Are intelligence agencies providing the types of flexible, telework, public transit–accessible workspaces that millennials desire?

In exit surveys of employees resigning from the IC in fiscal year 2013 (the most recent year for which data were available), the top two reasons civilian employees cited for leaving were lack of promotion opportunities (top response) and the availability of pay raises (second highest response).[18] Meanwhile, the top five reasons for resigning did not include work-life balance, workplace location, and the opportunity to work on challenging tasks. The IC is thus meeting millennial employees' needs in some areas but not others.

---

**Box 2**
**Millennials' Views on Flexible Workspaces**

- Forty-seven percent of U.S. millennials prefer the freedom to work and play from anywhere, at any time, with no restrictions, over a traditional 8-hours-a-day, Monday to Friday workweek.
- The employers of roughly one-quarter of millennials allow them to work from home; among these millennials, only 28 percent prefer to work in the office.
- Rather than driving cars, 14 percent of U.S. millennials commute to work by bus, subway, train, or walking.
- Fifty-five percent of U.S. millennials expect to have a higher salary in exchange for a longer commute.
- Two-thirds of millennials believe an organization that has adopted a flexible, mobile, and remote work model has a competitive advantage over one that requires employees to be in the office for 8 hours every weekday.
- Thirty-seven percent of U.S. millennials would accept a pay cut in exchange for greater flexibility; within that group, 25 percent would accept a cut greater than 20 percent of their salary.

SOURCE: Cisco Systems, "2014 Connected World Technology Final Report," San Jose, Calif., 2014.

---

[18] Office of the Director of National Intelligence, "IC Employee Exit Survey: FY13 Results Report," McLean, Va., May 2014, p. 19.

# CHAPTER FIVE

# Intelligence Community Gene Pool: Contractors, Researchers, Foreign Liaisons, and More

The IC gene pool includes potential employees the IC may wish to recruit today or in the future and millennial academics, businesspeople, contractors, and others whose skills, personal access, and information make them valuable candidate sources of information, subject-matter experts, advisors, and outside reviewers on issues of interest to the IC. Domestic and foreign business partners of the IC fall into this group because they provide continual opportunities for technological, substantive, and qualitative improvement, factors that may increase the depth of the IC gene pool.

Box 3 describes three subsegments of the IC gene pool. These groups include millennials who work in the IC as contractors, millennials from scientific and research

---

**Box 3**
**Subsegments of the IC Gene Pool**

**Green-Badged Millennials**

Millennials working as green-badged contractors in the IC share relationships with agencies similar to those of their federal civilian and military blue-badged counterparts, yet the IC does not control green-badge career development and workplace policies. Perceptions that green-badged employees are second-class citizens create morale, retention, and security risks that reverberate through agencies. Agencies should consider how they engage with these individuals.

**Scientists and Academics**

Researchers provide the IC with insights into innovative scientific and technological breakthroughs occurring in the United States and abroad, yet some scientists worry about how the government will use the information they provide. Engaging with this group provides opportunities to share information about how innovations are applied to improve national security.

**Foreign Partners and Liaisons**

IC agencies operate in foreign countries, where relationships with businesses and individuals are essential. Some foreign entities provide food, transportation, and logistics to employees and IC contractors overseas; other individuals and entities act as intelligence sources, foreign partners, and liaisons.

---

institutions who provide valuable information to the IC, and millennials in foreign countries who provide information or services to IC agencies.

Green-badged contractors have daily access to IC agencies and intimate understanding of IC missions and activities.[1] Millennials in this group may move between the green- and blue-badged workforces during their careers, making their career progression both nonlinear and extremely relevant to the IC's needs. As millennials have demonstrated a willingness to leave a job with higher pay and more security for one with more flexibility, more-interesting subject matter, and more-meaningful work, it has become common for green-badged millennials to move between contractor and government roles. The benefit this provides to the government is a workforce that has experienced a diverse set of roles and jobs across agencies and has a wide network of professional contacts and colleagues across agencies.

Yet because the IC does not control the hiring practices, employment policies, career development, mentoring, and supervision of these employees, the IC is heavily reliant on corporations to hire, train, retain, and develop workforces that will meet IC missions. Too often, agencies act as though keeping this workforce engaged and motivated is a purely corporate responsibility of the employer, yet when green-badge employees work full time in government offices, with government technology, under the direction of government program managers, on teams consisting of a mix of government personnel and contractors, it becomes the government's unofficial responsibility to manage this workforce and its morale. For these reasons, the ability to partner with contractors and keep them motivated and engaged is an Achilles' heel for the IC.

One striking similarity across surveys of millennials from around the world is their desire for businesses to partner with government to accomplish goals together. Millennials do not believe that government can solve problems by itself and do believe that partnerships are beneficial to accomplishing country-level goals. This perception could inspire millennials in the scientific and academic communities to partner and share information with the IC:

> While most Millennials believe business is having a positive impact on society by generating jobs (46 percent) and increasing prosperity (71 percent), they think business can do much more to address society's challenges in the areas of most concern: resource scarcity (56 percent), climate change (55 percent) and income equality (49 percent). Additionally, 50 percent of Millennials surveyed want to work for a business with ethical practices.[2]

Our research on millennials in the public revealed that many of them distrust the government and disagree with specific intelligence programs when revealed. The IC

---

[1]  In the intelligence community, government civilian and military employees are issued blue badges, while contractors are issued green badges.

[2]  Deloitte, 2014, p. 2.

gene pool is a subset of the public; therefore, the perceptions, mistrust, and fears of that group must be mitigated to grow the IC gene pool and continue keeping this population engaged. The IC has many opportunities to do this, and a proactive approach may be a factor in success.

Millennials believe that businesses should be driven by more than profits, and many millennials in the research sectors are pursing goals beyond profits. Scientists, academics, and other researchers act as subject-matter experts for the IC, providing information on specific topics, peer-reviewing IC assessments, and acting in advisory roles on boards and working groups that support specific intelligence topics. These roles align with millennials' perceptions that success should be measured in more than financial incentives:

> Millennials believe the success of a business should be measured in terms of more than just its financial performance, with a focus on improving society among the most important things it should seek to achieve. Millennials are also charitable and keen to participate in 'public life:' 63 percent of Millennials gave to charities, 43 percent actively volunteered or were a member of a community organization and 52 percent signed petitions.[3]

The IC has the opportunity to acknowledge and celebrate the benefits of partnerships, promoting the positive effects that partnerships with the commercial sector and research institutions have on national security. For U.S. millennials, this means the benefits these relationships have for U.S. security; for foreign millennials, this includes discussions about how the United States is helping local security and regional security stability.

The IC provides its business partners with the ability to advance national security, a tremendous goal, and a sense of accomplishment. The IC could shape the narrative describing the benefits of these relationships, thereby helping companies demonstrate to their own workforces, clients, and partners the companies' contributions to U.S. security. Without such messages coming from the IC, companies are too often left to reactively defend partnerships with the IC in the wake of bad publicity or intelligence leaks. The result is commercial partners that see relationships with the IC as part liability and part beneficial, rather than wholly beneficial.

Despite all its relationships with millennials in the commercial and research sectors, the IC could not accomplish its missions without foreign millennials to provide intelligence and other support on the ground around the world. Foreign nationals provide invaluable intelligence to IC agencies, either on their own or through their official roles as liaisons in foreign governments; work as translators and linguists; and filling local jobs, directly supporting U.S. intelligence functions. Foreign nationals in the

---

3   Deloitte, 2014, p. 3.

commercial sector provide the IC with intelligence collection, analysis, transportation, logistics, food, and other necessities in their local operating environments.

Cultivating and managing relationships with foreign national millennials in the IC gene pool is equally as essential to the IC as doing so in the United States. Millennials are rising faster in organizational structures in some countries than in others; around the world, millennials will have senior roles in every organization the IC will partner with. In Chapter Two, we learned that millennials in different regions will have different motivations for partnering with the IC. Therefore, the IC will need to tailor its relationships, communications, and agreements with foreign nationals according to their specific motivations and the needs of the agencies they work with.

Each of the different segments within the gene pool has distinct relationships with the IC that require unique information and methods of engagement. No one-size-fits-all approach will work across the IC gene pool. Different segments need different information from the IC, and the IC needs different information from each segment. Unique relationships will form within each segment and subsegment.

# CHAPTER SIX

# Conclusions

The bulk of current research on the millennial generation focuses on attitudes—what millennials think; what they believe; and what they say their wants, preferences, and motivations are. Less research has been done on behaviors—what millennials actually do, how they perform, or what drives them into or out of a workforce. Even less is known about the group of millennials that self-select to work for the government in general or the IC in particular.

Millennials' expectations about government and goals for their own careers warrant further research from intelligence agencies. While millennials have low trust in government and feel that government is unable to protect them, they also feel a responsibility to improve the public sector and believe that only government is positioned to respond to terrorism, war, and similar issues. Millennials believe that the public and private sectors have a responsibility to partner together to accomplish such goal. Millennials in both sectors may therefore feel incentivized to improve the relationship between these sectors with respect to intelligence sharing and partnerships.

The IC faces a decision about whether to either hire the best talent in the market or to hire only from the subset of the population that currently wants to work in intelligence and can pass the current security clearance screening process. Understanding the motivations that lure millennials into or drive them away from intelligence careers could be crucial to IC leaders and human resources professionals alike. However, the IC has neither closely studied the perspectives of millennials who have self-selected to work in the IC nor developed an understanding of the appeal or lack of appeal of intelligence career fields to the millennial generation.

Research and analysis on how millennials' perceptions of the IC differ from those of other generations is nearly nonexistent, and we found insufficient data to examine and comprehensively understand how to engage millennials in intelligence across the four segments. The IC has an opportunity to affect the success of intelligence missions and functions in the future by creating thoughtful approaches to engaging this population that align intelligence goals with millennials' goals and values.

# CHAPTER SEVEN

# Areas for Further Research

We have explored the literature and current research on the millennial generation in an attempt to focus the issues the IC faces and to suggest how the IC should engage millennials across multiple segments to succeed with them in the future. Additional research and analysis inside the IC would enable leaders to make informed decisions as they begin to wrestle with such questions as the following:

- How can agencies create workplaces that attract millennial talent in all fields? When millennials have chosen not to apply for intelligence careers, what were their reasons? How do these decisions affect intelligence agencies?
- How can agencies retain millennials throughout their career paths? Or, alternatively, how can agencies provide opportunities for millennials to enter and exit intelligence career paths throughout their careers?
- How do millennials' perceptions of and willingness to partner with intelligence agencies differ by race, ethnicity, gender, sexual orientation, parental status, and other demographic elements?
- How do agencies create engagement strategies for millennial contractors and researchers to promote collaboration? What motivations or nonfinancial incentives would encourage such collaboration?
- How might engagements with foreign liaisons change when millennials fill these roles overseas? What motivations or nonfinancial incentives would encourage such collaboration?
- How do millennial clients expect to receive intelligence and integrate it into their decisionmaking? How do these expectations differ from current intelligence production and dissemination practices, and what can the IC do to close the gap?
- How will intelligence providers contribute to the team-oriented environment that millennial clients will lead?
- How could agencies engage with the U.S. public to generate trust in IC missions and capabilities? How would agencies measure the effectiveness of such programs?
- How are agencies generating trust overseas with millennials in the foreign public and in foreign governments to promote information sharing with these governments?

# Abbreviations

| | |
|---|---|
| CIA | Central Intelligence Agency |
| FARC | Revolutionary Armed Forces of Colombia |
| IC | intelligence community |
| IT | information technology |
| NATO | North Atlantic Treaty Organization |
| NSA | National Security Agency |
| STEM | science, technology, engineering, and mathematics |
| UK | United Kingdom |

# Bibliography

Air Force Instruction 36-2903, *Dress and Personal Appearance of Air Force Personnel*, July 18, 2011.

Army Regulation 670-1, *Wear and Appearance of Army Uniforms and Insignia*,"April 10, 2015.

American Press Institute, "How Millennials Get News: Inside the Habits of America's First Digital Generation," March 16, 2015. As of April 28, 2016:
http://www.americanpressinstitute.org/publications/reports/survey-research/millennials-news/single-page/

Brady, Diane, "Millennials Descend on Canada's Parliament," *Bloomberg Businessweek*, May 19, 2011. As of April 28, 2016:
http://www.bloomberg.com/news/articles/2011-05-19/millennials-descend-on-canadas-parliament

Briggs, Craig, and Kathryn Sloane, "What Do Asia's Millennials See Ahead?" *Marketing Daily*, August 20, 2013. As of April 28, 2016:
http://www.mediapost.com/publications/article/205771/what-do-asias-millennials-see-ahead.html

Burstein, David D., "Innovation Agents: Oscar Morales and One Million Voices Against FARC," *Fast Company*, May 21, 2012. As of April 28, 2016:
http://www.fastcompany.com/1836318/innovation-agents-oscar-morales-and-one-million-voices-against-farc

———, *Fast Future: How the Millennial Generation Is Shaping Our World*, Boston: Beacon Press, 2013.

Carlisle, Nate, "Shutting off NSA's water gains support in Utah Legislature," *Salt Lake Tribune*, November 19, 2014. As of April 28, 2016:
http://www.sltrib.com/news/politics/1845843-155/data-utah-bill-nsa-center-committee?fullpage=1

Cisco Systems, "2014 Connected World Technology Final Report," San Jose, Calif., 2014. As of April 28, 2016:
http://www.cisco.com/c/dam/en/us/solutions/collateral/enterprise/connected-world-technology-report/cisco-2014-connected-world-technology-report.pdf

Clapper, James, "Current and Projected Security Threats Against the United States," testimony before the Select Committee on Intelligence, U.S. Senate, Washington D.C., January 29, 2014.

Cole, Juan, *The New Arabs: How the Millennial Generation Is Changing the Middle East*, New York: Simon & Schuster, 2014.

Cone Inc., "The Millennial Generation: Pro-Social and Empowered to Change the World," 2006. As of April 28, 2016:
http://www.greenbook.org/Content/AMP/Cause_AMPlified.pdf

Congressional Budget Office, "Comparing the Compensation of Federal and Private-Sector Employees," Washington, D.C., Pub. No. 4403, January 2012. As of April 28, 2016:
http://www.cbo.gov/publication/42921?index=12696

Council of Economic Advisors, "15 Economic Facts About Millennials," Washington, D.C., Executive Office of the President, October 2014. As of January 29, 2016:
https://www.whitehouse.gov/sites/default/files/docs/millennials_report.pdf

Czekalinski, Stephanie, and Ronald Brownstein, "What It's Like to Be a Millennial in Congress," *National Journal*, June 5, 2014. As of April 28, 2016:
http://www.nationaljournal.com/magazine/what-it-s-like-to-be-a-millennial-in-congress-20140605

Davis, Jack, "Tensions in Analyst-Policymaker Relations: Opinions, Facts, and Evidence," The Sherman Kent Center for Intelligence Analysis, Central Intelligence Agency website, January 2003. As of April 28, 2016:
https://www.cia.gov/library/kent-center-occasional-papers/vol2no2.htm

Deal, Jennifer J., David G. Altman, and Steven G. Rogelberg, "Millennials at Work: What We Know and What We Need to Do (If Anything)," *Journal of Business and Psychology*, Vol. 25, No. 2, June 2010, pp. 191–199. As of April 8, 2016:
http://www.jstor.org/stable/40605778?seq=2#page_scan_tab_contents

Deloitte, "Big Demands and High Expectations: The Deloitte Millennial Survey," New York, January 2014. As of April 28, 2016:
https://www2.deloitte.com/content/dam/Deloitte/global/Documents/About-Deloitte/gx-dttl-2014-millennial-survey-report.pdf

Director of National Intelligence, *The National Intelligence Strategy of the United States of America*, Washington, D.C., 2014. As of April 28, 2016:
https://www.dni.gov/files/documents/2014_NIS_Publication.pdf

Fish, Eric, *China's Millennials: The Want Generation,* Lanham, Md.: Rowman & Littlefield, June 4, 2015.

Fry, Richard, "Millennials Overtake Baby Boomers as America's Largest Generation," Pew Research Center website, April 25, 2016. As of May 4, 2016:
http://www.pewresearch.org/fact-tank/2016/04/25/millennials-overtake-baby-boomers/

Gorman, Phil, Teresa Nelson, and Alan Glassman, "The Millennial Generation: A Strategic Opportunity," *Organizational Analysis*, Vol. 12, No. 3, July 2004, pp. 255–270.

Institute of Politics, "While Edward Snowden's Legacy May Be An Open Question Among Millennials, Collecting Personal Information for National Security Is Not," Cambridge, Mass.: Harvard University, undated. As of April 28, 2016:
http://www.iop.harvard.edu/while-edward-snowden%E2%80%99s-legacy-may-be-open-question-among-millennials-collecting-personal-information

Institute of Politics, "Trust in Institutions and the Political Process," web page, Cambridge, Mass.: Harvard University, 2014a. As of March 15, 2016:
http://www.iop.harvard.edu/trust-institutions-and-political-process

Institute of Politics, "Survey of Young Americans' Attitudes Toward Politics and Public Service," 25th ed., Cambridge, Mass.: Harvard University, April 29, 2014b. As of December 4, 2015:
http://www.iop.harvard.edu/sites/default/files_new/Harvard_ExecSummarySpring2014.pdf

Hauslohner, Abigail, "Young Russians Never Knew the Soviet Union, but They Hope to Recapture Days of Its Empire," *Washington Post*, June 10, 2014. As of April 28, 2016:
http://www.washingtonpost.com/world/europe/young-russians-never-knew-the-soviet-union-but-they-hope-to-recapture-days-of-its-empire/2014/06/09/66a3e1a4-684a-4ab8-9261-04b7d1b59dad_story.html

Hershatter, Andrea, and Molly Epstein, "Millennials and the World of Work: An Organization and Management Perspective," *Journal of Business and Psychology*, Vol. 25, No. 2, June 2010, pp. 211–223. As of April 28, 2016:
http://rd.springer.com/article/10.1007%2Fs10869-010-9160-y

Hooton, Christopher, "Our Attention Span Is Now Less Than That of a Goldfish, Microsoft Study Finds," *Independent*, May 13, 2015. As of April 28, 2016:
http://www.independent.co.uk/news/science/our-attention-span-is-now-less-than-that-of-a-goldfish-microsoft-study-finds-10247553.html

Kent, Brendan, "Millennial Must-Read: Defining Pussy Riot," Cambridge, Mass.: Institute of Politics, Harvard University, 2014.

Levenson, Alec, "Millennials and the World of Work: An Economist's Perspective," *Journal of Business and Psychology*, Vol. 25, No. 2, 2010, pp. 257–264. As of April 28, 2016:
http://rd.springer.com/article/10.1007%2Fs10869-010-9170-9

Marine Admin Message 198/07, "Amplification to the Marine Corps Tattoo Policy," January 15, 2010.

Martin, Carol A., "From High Maintenance to High Productivity: What Managers Need to Know About Generation Y," *Industrial and Commercial Training*, Vol. 37, No. 1, 2005, pp. 39–44.

McMillan, Robert, "Utah Considers Cutting off Water to the NSA's Monster Data Center," *Wired*, November 20, 2014. As of April 28, 2016:
http://www.wired.com/2014/11/utah-considers-cutting-water-nsas-monster-data-center/

McCrindle, Mark, "Superannuation and the Under 40s," summary report, Bella Vista NSW, Australia: McCrindle Research, July 18, 2005.

Meek, Teresa, "Global Survey: Today's Millennials Are Tech-Savvy, Footloose, Confident and Practical," Coca-Cola Journey website, October 13, 2014. As of April 28, 2016:
http://www.coca-colacompany.com/stories/global-survey-todays-millennials-are-tech-savvy-footloose-confident-and-practical

Microsoft Canada, "Attention Spans: Consumer Insights," Spring 2015. As of May 4, 2016:
https://advertising.microsoft.com/en/WWDocs/User/display/cl/researchreport/31966/en/microsoft-attention-spans-research-report.pdf

"Millennials and News, Fact-Checked," YPulse website, May 29, 2013.

Milligan, Susan, "Capturing the Wisdom of Four Generations," *HR Magazine*, Vol. 59 No. 11, November 2014. As of April 28, 2016:
https://www.shrm.org/publications/hrmagazine/editorialcontent/2014/1114/pages/1114-intergenerational-knowledge-transfer.aspx

MSLGroup, "Asian Millennials Expect Business to Solve Important Social Issues and Empower Gen Y to Drive Change Together," web page, September 17, 2014. As of April 28, 2016:
http://asia.mslgroup.com/news/asian-millennials-expect-business-to-solve-important-social-issues-and-empower-gen-y-to-drive-change-together/

Myers, Karen K., and Kamyab Sadaghiani, "Millennials in the Workplace: A Communication Perspective on Millennials' Organizational Relationships and Performance," *Journal of Business and Psychology*, Vol. 25, No. 2, June 2010, pp. 225–238.

National Intelligence Council, *Global Trends 2030: Alternative Worlds*, Washington, D.C., December 2012.

Navy Administrative Instruction 110/06, Amplifies the Navy's Personal Appearance Policy with regards to tattoos, body art, brands, mutilations and dental ornamentation, October 1, 2003.

Office of the Director of National Intelligence, "IC Employee Exit Survey: FY13 Results Report," McLean, Va., May 2014.

Pew Research Center, *Millennials: A Portrait of Generation Next: Confident. Connected. Open to Change*, Washington, D.C., February 2010. As of January 29, 2016:
http://www.pewsocialtrends.org/files/2010/10/millennials-confident-connected-open-to-change.pdf.

———, "Amid Criticism, Support for Media's 'Watchdog' Role Stands Out," August 8, 2013. As of May 17, 2016:
http://www.people-press.org/2013/08/08/
amid-criticism-support-for-medias-watchdog-role-stands-out/

———, "Generations and Issues," in Pew Research Center, *Millennials in Adulthood: Detached from Institutions, Networked with Friends*, March 7, 2014a. As of April 28, 2016:
http://www.pewsocialtrends.org/files/2014/03/2014-03-07_generations-report-version-for-web.pdf

———, "About Half See CIA Interrogation Methods as Justified," web page, December 15, 2014b. As of March 10, 2016:
http://www.people-press.org/2014/12/15/about-half-see-cia-interrogation-methods-as-justified/

PNC, "PNC Financial Independence Survey—Part II: A National Study of the Financial Behaviors of 20-Somethings," March 2012. As of April 28, 2016:
https://www.pnc.com/content/dam/pnc-com/pdf/aboutpnc/PressKits/
FinancialIndependenceSurvey/2012_March_FinInd%20Overview.pdf

Poulsen, Kevin, "Apple's iPhone Encryption Is a Godsend, Even if Cops Hate It," *Wired*, October 8, 2014. As of April 28, 2016:
http://www.wired.com/2014/10/golden-key/

PricewaterhouseCoopers, "Millennials at Work: Reshaping the Workplace," New York, 2011. As of April 28, 2016:
www.pwc.com/en_M1/m1/services/consulting/documents/millennials-at-work.pdf

Rohani, Afshin, "A State of Unrest: Iran's Youth Face Unemployment and Rising Apathy," *Urban Times*, June 19, 2014.

Ryan, Kellie, "Lessons from the Survey: Millennials Grow More Partisan, Think Washington Is Broken," Cambridge, Mass.: Institute of Politics, Harvard University, May 7, 2013.

Stafford, Darlene E., and Henry S. Griffis, *A Review of Millennial Generation Characteristics and Military Workforce Implications*, Alexandria, Virginia: The CNA Corporation, CRM D0018211.A1/ Final, May 31, 2008. As of December 9, 2015:
https://www.cna.org/CNA_files/PDF/D0018211.A1.pdf

Stilwell, Victoria, "Millennials Most-Educated U.S. Age Group After Downturn: Economy," Bloomberg Markets website, October 8, 2014. As of April 28, 2016:
http://www.bloomberg.com/news/articles/2014-10-08/
millennials-become-most-educated-u-s-age-group-due-to-recession

Stokes, Bruce, "Who Are Europe's Millennials?" Washington, D.C.: Pew Research Center, February 9, 2015. As of April 28, 2016:
http://www.pewresearch.org/fact-tank/2015/02/09/who-are-europes-millennials/

Strauss, William, and Neil Howe, *Millennials Rising: The Next Great Generation*, New York: Vintage Books, 2000.

Taylor, Paul, *The Next America*, New York: Public Affairs, 2014.

Telefónica, "Telefónica Global Millennial Survey: Focus on Global," fact sheet, undated. As of April 28, 2016:
http://survey.telefonica.com/portfolio/global-results-fact-sheet/

Telefónica, "Global Millennial Survey: Global Results," website, 2013a. As of April 28, 2016:
http://survey.telefonica.com/globalreports/

————, "Middle East & Africa: What Makes Millennials Tick?" November 28, 2013b. As of April 28, 2016:
http://www.slideshare.net/TelefonicaEurope/tef-mea-millennialstick112213

————, "European Millennials," *Telefónica Global Millennial Survey*, 2014. As of April 28, 2016:
http://survey.telefonica.com/meet-the-millennials/europe/

"Think You Know the Next Gen Investor?" *UBS Investor Watch*, January 12, 2016. As of April 28, 2016:
https://www.ubs.com/microsites/ubs-investor-watch/en/millennial-attitudes.html

Twenge, Jean M., "A Review of the Empirical Evidence on Generational Differences in Work Attitudes," *Journal of Business and Psychology*, Vol. 25, No. 2, 2010, pp. 201–210. As of June 15, 2016:
http://www.scopus.com/inward/record.url?eid=2-s2.0-77952419177&partnerID=40&md5=f4dac74aa52b304cd211d2434a66469

Twenge, Jean M., Stacy M. Campbell, Brian J. Hoffman, and Charles E. Lance, "Generational Differences in Work Values: Leisure and Extrinsic Values Increasing, Social and Intrinsic Values Decreasing," *Journal of Management*, Vol. 36, No. 5, 2010, pp. 1117–1142. As of June 15, 2016:
http://www.scopus.com/inward/record.url?eid=2-s2.0-77952419136&partnerID=40&md5=20dbc1856344c5b90647c2db61afffc5

U.S. Census Bureau, "Table 1. Population by Age and Sex: 2012," *Age and Sex Composition in the United States*, 2012. As of April 28, 2016:
https://www.census.gov/population/age/data/2012comp.html

————, "American Community Survey: 2009–2013," CB14-219, 2014. As of April 28, 2016:
https://www.census.gov/data/developers/data-sets/acs-survey-5-year-data.html

————, "Language Other than English Spoken at Home, Age 18 to 34," graphic, undated. As of February 2015:
http://census.socialexplorer.com/young-adults/#/report/quick/nation/US/language-other-than-english-spoken-at-home-age-18-to-34

Willyerd, Karie, "Social Tools Can Improve Employee Onboarding," *Harvard Business Review*, December 21, 2012.

World Economic Forum, "Survey Results 2015: Global Shapers Community," 2015.